77 poems from a Philadelphia garden

Aron Goldschneider
隆雪瀧

Drinking Wine (飲酒)

I have built my house
Right where others dwell

Yet free from the din
Of horse and carriage

You ask, sir,
How can it be so?

With heart and mind
Untroubled by self

I pluck a chrysanthemum
By the garden's eastern hedge

And gaze at ease
On mountains to the south

From which the finest air
Flows day and night

And birds gather
To fly home

Therein lies an essence
I have lost words to convey

陶淵明
Tao Yuan Ming
(A.D. 365–427)

(translated by the author)

77 poems from a Philadelphia garden

poems by Aron Goldschneider
illustrations by Bronwyn Goldschneider

UN·BAN BOOKS Philadelphia,
Pennsylvania

77 Poems From a Philadelphia Garden
First Edition, Un-Ban Books 2025

www.arongoldschneider.com
For more information: 77gardenpoems@gmail.com

Illustrations	Bronwyn Goldschneider
Book design	Margherita Buzzi
	Bronwyn Goldschneider
	Aron Goldschneider
Typesetting	Margherita Buzzi

Typeset in Source Han Serif SC

Special thanks to Philip Kay for his helpful
suggestions.

**UN·BAN
BOOKS**

Library of Congress Control
Number: 2025902274
ISBN(Paperback): 979-8-9884117-0-3
ISBN(eBook): 979-8-9884117-1-0

Un–Ban Books
Philadelphia, Pennsylvania USA

Author's note

For seven years, I joyfully toiled in a beautiful and historic
Philadelphia garden, caring for it and making it my own. As my
feelings for the garden deepened, I began to write poems that I
felt might speak to the souls of my fellow gardeners.

A humble, lifelong student of the Chinese language, I was aware
that I was completing this collection of garden poems just as
"Chinese Valentine's Day" or "Double Seven" was arriving on
the seventh day of the seventh month of the Chinese lunisolar
calendar. On this special day in August, the celestial Cowherd
and Weaving Maid are said to meet in the heavens.

It seemed like kismet that I had written about 77 poems. So I
titled the work *77 Poems From a Philadelphia Garden* and teamed
up with my daughter Bronwyn to create this illustrated book.
We hope that anyone who has ever worked or wandered in a
garden will enjoy it.

Table of contents

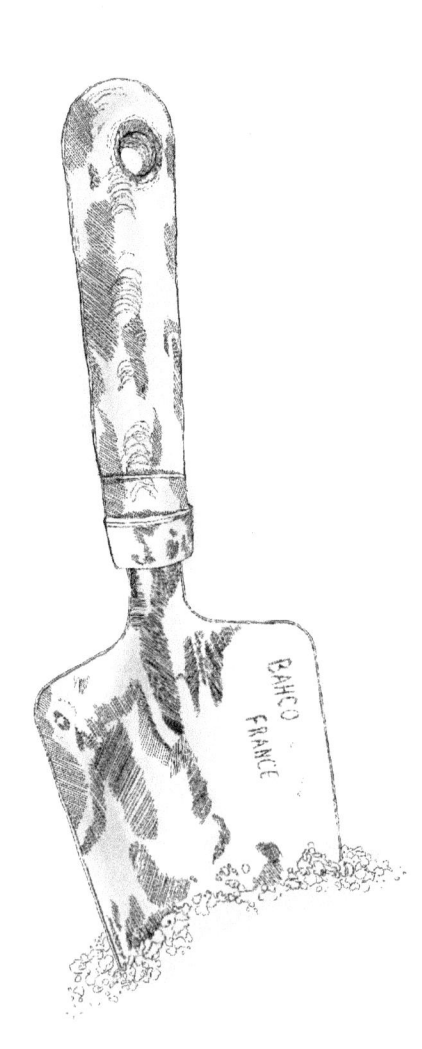

Spade

When I took rein
Of this garth

Seven long years ago
This July

The ghost owners
Had left me a spade

Not casually placed
Upon a table or a stone

But standing starkly upright
In a raised bed

As if pitched in place
For the last time

Perhaps a spade
Was just a spade

Or better yet a friendly
Handing of the baton

Yet I must say,
As years of toil and joy have passed

I am put in mind
Of John Henry

Who laid down his hammer
By the side of the road
Painted in red

Snake Handling

I like how
Fresh rubber snakes
Feel in my hands

I like coiling them
On the fig trees
To set the stage for Eve

Or on the lattice
Of the grape arbor
To pose a new Canaan

Sometimes I leave them
Writhing
In the grass
To ward sparrows
Off the seed

Or place their
Diamond heads
By a chipmunk's hole
To keep foolery
Shining

Alongside Me

Back among the stems and shoots
Cradled by the rustle
Of the leaves

I felt in company
Of a loving family
And I asked myself,

Isn't the most cherished
She who bears fruit for the hungry,
Nurtures, and shelters from wind and rain?

I've heard it said:

And yet

They are faithful
When others abandon

They abide
Where others abscond

They embrace
When others turn away

It is to them I shall give my love

They do not move
They are planted
They do not speak
They are dumb
They do not feel
They are stolid

Ode to Lesser Celandine

Dearest Celandine,

You appear as of once,
Precisely everywhere
That I don't want you.

Wherever the sun shines
And a drink may be had,
There you are.

Intruding on conversations,
You crowd out beauty
And make a nuisance of yourself.

I am not fooled
By your dainty yellow flowers
That charm my wife.

Nor by the blessed fact
That you are ephemeral
And disappear before summer,

As I know
Each year there is more of you,
And then again

Still more of you,

Until

There is only you.

Silver Lining-notes

The eyesorious hemlock
is dead as a doornail

The arborist left us a half-severed stub[1]

The autumn joy sedum
has wrestler's ears

Her succulent lobes chewed down to the nub[2]

The hedges are laden
with runners and creepers

Only merciless privet could stand such abuse[3]

By the side of the house
In forgotten places

Ferns grow tall and weeds are profuse[4]

[1] Woodpeckers come to tap on the beam,
[2] Hollywood finches are vegan it seems,
[3] Cardinal fledglings are safe in its shade,
[4] Deep in the tangle, a dove nest is laid.

Norway Be Gone

When the hardy and wicked Norway maple was cut down and stumped,
The chestnut sighed, spread its wings, and flowered with glee.
A competitor gone, a shadow caster destroyed,
It was so joyful, it weeped liquid from its side.
Reigning as of old, unchallenged, with leafy crown restored to glory,
The furrowed tree bore well the burning sun, the dearth of rain,
And raised its burly arms in praise,
Staying green like a hallelujah right through the summer.
For long and bitter years, its cry had gone unheeded,
"Who will rid me of this meddlesome Norway?"
Enmity deep within the rings of its core.
But now, honeyed life had come again, and
The air was sweet with the death of another.

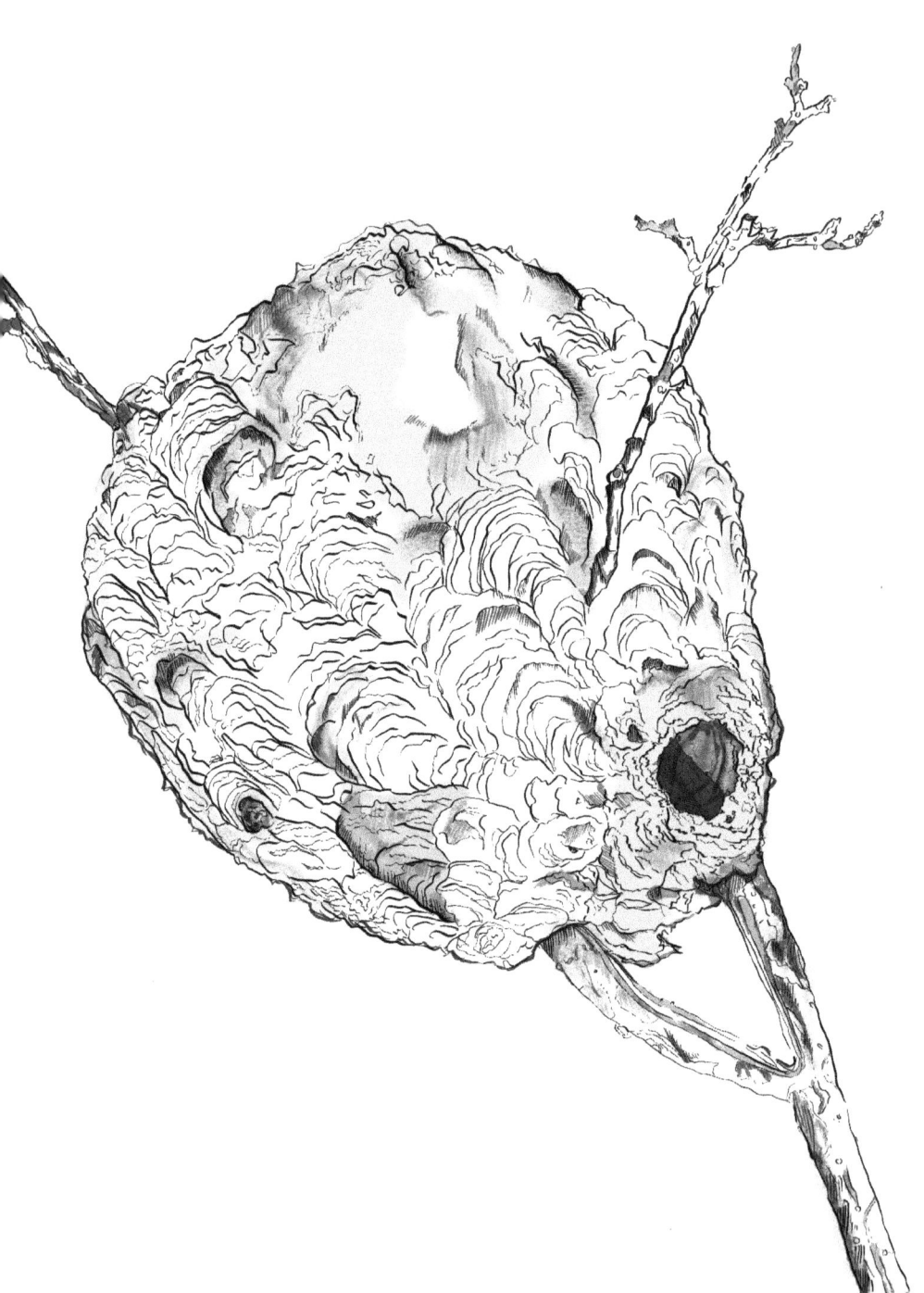

Lady Garden

Mosquitoes have bled me
A thousand times
I bend the knee
And mind them not

Long days in the sun
Have left me wrinkled
Use me dear lady
I will not yield

Hornets have stung me
On my face, my hands
Your humble servant
I am not deterred

Wind and hail
A life in seasons
Attending you only
My honor and joy

Personal Growth

In spite of my misguided opinions
stupid prejudices
and failure to moderate
my language

The crocuses push their way up each year

And while I have not adjusted
to modern sensitivities
nor jettisoned
my reverence for the outdated and lame

The shrubs ignore my shortcomings

At sunset
the wind blows gently
the door is ajar
and I'm safely in the ground

Your Garden Shoes

Your garden shoes,
Left by the door,
Fill me with longing and tenderness.

So diminutive and childlike,
They rest there, asking nothing, telling nothing,
Like an only child, alone unto herself, needing no one.

Tell me.
Do you leave them there like the cicada husks,
That even now, you never fail to examine
To see
If the strange seven-year body of the cicada is really gone?

And when, by surprise, the cicada is still turning within,
Could it be that you gently place it on a tree,
With such care and kindness,
Because it was once the best playmate of a lonely country girl?

Turnip Greens

A goldfinch
Returning of an afternoon once again
To taste that morning's turnip greens

Perched, and as is that finch's wont
Surveyed at length the ground below,
Bright plumage calling for
A cautious approach

But like a heartstruck lover
Pausing each day to steal a glance
Through the windows of a café
Where she once worked

He found nothing there,
Nothing as it had been

And no matter how he flitted
To and fro
And cocked his little crown
Wondering, wondering

The image in his mind

Filed away for reference

Cherished and stored

Would not match up
With the barren sight
Meeting his sharp little eyes

Alas, what he could not know,
Need not know
Was that I had spent the afternoon
Alone with his greens

Cooking them tenderly
Ever so gently

Savoring them and enjoying them for myself

Line of Descent

Are my parents sleeping
With the spiders
In the damp, decaying corner by the shed?

Or are their spirits flitting about
Like the twig in the wren's mouth?

Did they grow hard when they left me?
Mineral rich, like quartz?

Or do they flow like rivulets
Di Di Da Da
Down the glossy window pane?

Gathering leaves in the muck,
I reflect on another season of scintillating achievement.
How proud they must be!

"My Garden"

Why am I out there
You ask
Weary, itching, wet and dry
In all manner of weather?

Perhaps to be present

When silent nests
So finely built and tended
Stir with untried life

When a murder of crows
Drive a hawk
From the land

When creatures uncovered
Wriggle and scurry in
The leaf litter

When what grows and dies away
Provides a passing illusion
Of "my garden"

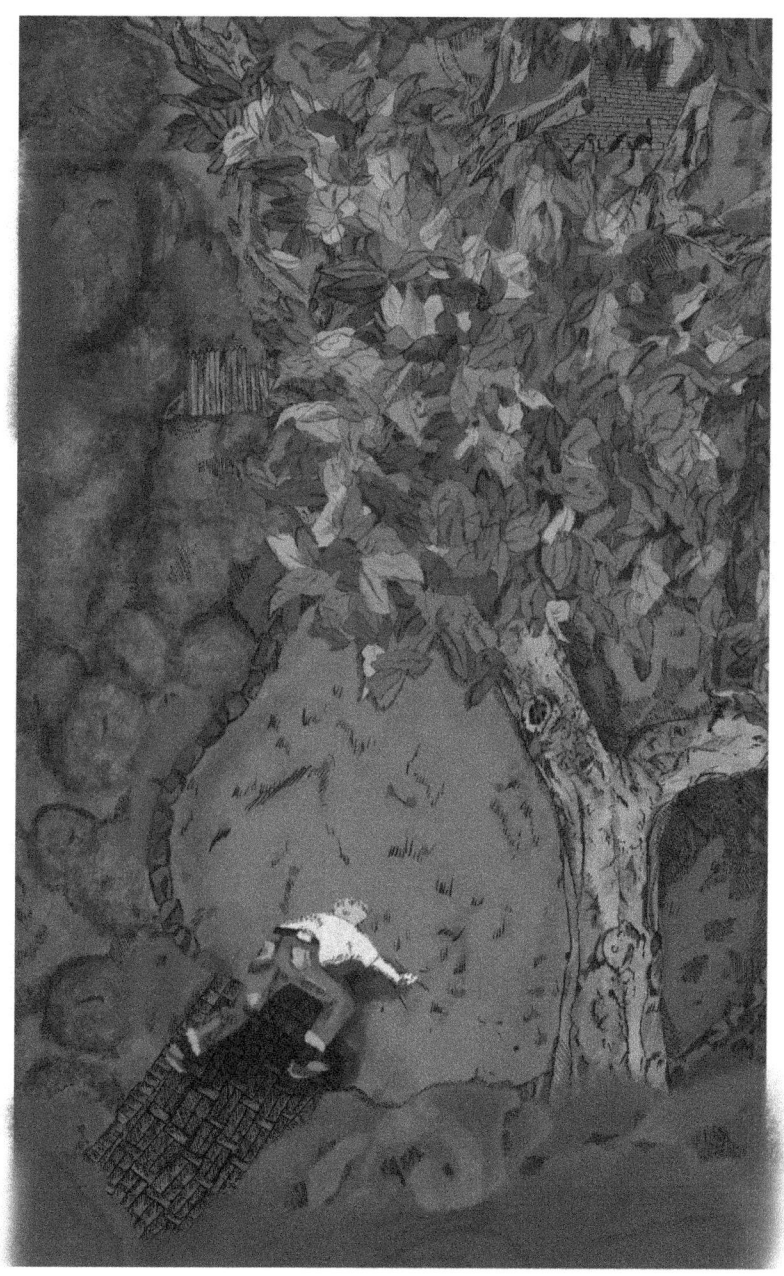

Neighbors

Ivy spilling over the fence
Bamboo breaching the party line

Neighbors

His extension cord runs free
Why is it on my side?

Neighbors

Countless hours pulling the noxious, iron-rooted
"flowering ground cover" that the garden center
sold her

Neighbors

Weed killer drifting by
Fourth time I've gathered their leaves

Neighbors

Begging for them to prune their trees
And then paying for half of it

Neighbors

Screen door slamming in and out
His mower sounds like a jet landing

Neighbors

Precious cries of "hide and seek"
Sweet home cooking on the breeze

Gotta love them neighbors

Self-sustaining

Some years back
I knew a young, troubled man named Will
Who was much grateful for a bookcase
I was giving away

And while we were carrying it
Through the vegetable garden
And he wondered at the space
And number of beds

He remarked, in his manic,
Neo-hippy voice,
"Wow, you could be self-sustaining!"

A week or two later,
I heard the news that he had overdosed,
Taking his young life.

I wondered if there were more
That could have sustained him.

Intimations

Sullied snow
Aged beyond its time of beauty

Maps the unseen,
Providing notice that

A hungry fox
Circled through the garden,

A passerby's dog
Pissed on our gate,

And Mr. Squirrel has been
At it again
With the bird feeder.

Now, in the cold early morning,
As I gaze out the back window,
I even begin to see

The generous footprints
Left by the soft feet of the llama

That as yet
My wife only dreams of.

Rumbling

Sometimes distant rumbling means
Rain is falling elsewhere

Softly drifting mizzle
Is a luxury indeed

Anytime the lightning strikes
I like tall things around me

Downpours channel where they will
Making riverboats of leaves

隆隆

有時遙遠隆隆
意味
雨他方下來

輕輕游移毛毛雨
珍貴得奢麗

隨時隨地雷擊
喜歡被比我高的東西圍繞

暴雨灌輪揮灑
讓葉子成為航船

Lacuna

Inasmuch as
I have seen
Death
I have seen
The middle place
Where people go
Before they die

A place where
The world's concerns
And all that we hold dear
Sights, smells, sounds
May grow distant or
Bothersome to the traveler

And I wonder if perhaps
The more lasting memory
To linger
When I one day walk
That lonesome valley

May not be the taste of any
Ripened tomato
On my tongue

Nor tender fig
Down my gullet

But rather
The acrid odor
Of tomato vines
On my fingers

The pissy scent
Of fig leaves
On the breeze

Adoration

Flower ladies crouching on kneelers
Sweaty moonfaces upturned
Beatific smiles on their lips

Old fuddy-duddy grandpas
Hiking belly-high shorts over
Calf-hugging nylons

Everyone wearing netting hats
Smelling vaguely medicinal
Like wet magnolia petals

Everyone nursing aches and pains
Soldiering on
In the sun's bending time

Heroes of compost and coffee

Heroes of bees and basil

Heroes of not giving a damn

My heroes

Tall Pines

Today I heard the tall pines
Creaking in the cold
And I felt the fragileness of things

When the sun shines on me
I consider that I may be loved

Certainly I have been a most lucky
And fortunate man

But I guess my feelings on the matter
Have always been
That it would be presumptuous of me to assume
A personal relationship with the Almighty

It is to this outlook that I feel I owe my luck

參天松樹

今天我聽到了
參天松樹
在冷空氣裡嘰嘰嘎嘎
覺得萬物很易碎

太陽光下在我身上的時候
讓思考可能被愛

確實我是個非常幸運的人

但猜我對它的長期感覺是
假設跟老天有私人的關係太非分了

覺得運道是這個看法的產物

Pike 矛

When rain
Is absent
I must water

Shield 盾

When rain
Is ample
I must weed

Slumbrous

When I was a young man
I read many books

In English
My native tongue

Late into evenings
Late into nights

Now it seems
I read little

But the garden

As the night-light
Bothers you

And I fall asleep
On the pages

Dull and drowsing
A head filled with stems
A head full of petals

Sunlight and soil
Scuttling vermin
Fluttering birds

The boredom of the hound

The Browning

I had a neighbor once
Who was a gardener
Because he charged folks money

Sometimes I'd see him alarmed—
He'd left his "deep watering" running
The homeowner's garden was now a lake

He liked to gab with my helpers
When they were on the clock
And a deadline loomed

Most assuredly argued
Round Up's safety
And sprayed it maskless like a champ

He favored hosta
Not for the hummingbirds
But because it was foolproof

Yet much of what he planted
Died
There was no love in it

His own garden was tended by his wife
She would not let him touch it
Anyway, her name was on the deed

He had no truck
So he never made the transition
Half-measures it was, but he thought he was a gift

I think of him from time to time
In the hard parts of my garden
When disease and pestilence arise
Or my fingers won't go down in the clay

Stillness

While sweeping
The mossy bricks
Of the middle garden

I sometimes peer into
The house
Where we live

As if peering into
A doll's house

At someone else's things
At someone else's stillness

As if I were the garden

51

Tombak

When I stand
In the garden
And embrace
Rain's arrival

My senses drink in
Her quickening gift

A murmuring to the ears
A pattering on the skin

Leaf and petal
Yet unladen
At play

Uncle Observes

Yesterday I saw a fledgling song sparrow
Tottering along the dog-eared pickets
Buzzing and chirping for his mother
Like a teenager demanding a meal

Yet I, like a tough-love uncle,
Observed that this lad quite readily could fly
When he fluttered down to the ground
And randomly pecked at sundry twigs

Observed that he flew quite capably
Onto the neighbor's garage
To make a further spectacle
Of his begging and pleading

Observed that when mother returned
He readily traversed the mossy roof
Clambering at her with such noisy force
That I feared he would harm her

Observed how cloddish and crude
He behaved next to mother
And how ungrateful he was
For the bug down his gullet

Observed with bemusement
My own reproving words—
"Just one day more of this, bud.
Tomorrow you will be on your own."

Spotted Lanternfly

Like a robin's clumsy fluttering
Your flight is direct, desperate, and stupid:
Utterly lacking in evasiveness or undulation

You are no butterfly or goldfinch

Yet as no birds choose to eat you
We gardeners are directed by the authorities
To kill you[1]

I am no Jainist
My very soles have crushed millions
And yet

The beautiful red of your inner wings
Is all that is needed
To awaken

Regret

Your woody surface
Crafted by God himself
To mimic bark

Arouses sympathy[2]

Incant—

"Lizard's tail and bishop's weed,
Lanternfly and slug,
How I love you,
How I kill you,
Let me count the ways"

[1] Pol Pots—required
[2] Flower Pots—optional

Modern Man

As my fingers perform
The ancient ritual of
Pressing
My bean seeds
An inch down in the soil

My voice speaks into
A nestled earbud
Passing
My "懷古的話"

8,000 miles through the Earth

Ignorante

Don't know pH
The hydrangeas are blue

Never sprayed Roundup
Got hands to pull

No 10-10-10
I can pee in a jug

Cut the plum down
If it don't give me plums

Yesterday and Today

Anaerobic soil

Non-native invasives

Phosphorous deficiency

pH imbalance

YESTERDAY'S GARDEN

Drunkenness

Cheap bastid owes me

Hungry-ass poor people

Sadness

TODAY'S GARDEN

Body dysmorphia

Generalized anxiety

Sexual addiction

Food insecurity

Overgrown

Poor soil

Dense shade

Soggy

Sleeping Garden

A scrap of wood sits alone on the slate table
Hanging out for no apparent reason
He's too diminutive to be a stake
Yet my hands left him there
So I find his uselessness lovable.

Pushing up through the heavy snow
A few mysterious objects
"Better brought inside"
Perhaps suggest a purpose
Or not
But I left them there
And no one could tell me not to.

Butt-cold chairs,
Once here
Now there
Backwards, unpaired
Facing nowhere
Wrong? I say not.

I like their randomness.
As if random people were sitting in them.
It's my randomness.

Traces

On Tuesday, I found
by my escarole
a little porcelain hand
disembodied from a doll
left by Franklin Smith's daughter
on a Wednesday in 1845.

Three years ago,
I resurrected
Minnie McCammon's
Celtic Cross,
dropped like an anchor
in the deep soil of the middle garden.

Last night, I plaster cast the footprints
trodden by a thief named Winslow
in the crime-ridden 70's,
when he traversed the lawn,
scaled the back roof,
and entered the house thusly.

Just this past decade, I uncovered
a jasper turtleback scraper
that a Lenni Lenape named "Forgetful One"
used to skin a deer here
but misplaced
on maple-sap-rising day.

Then, to celebrate July Fourth,
I smoked a joint with the boat maker Wright,
who made his home here in the 1950's,
and we chuckled at the humorously crude carpentry
that defines the rudimentary shelves and sills
of the tool garage, which began as a stable.

While on humid August nights, I still hear
the eerie half-bark of the fox
who sheltered her kits
by the yard's back corner
and devoured the ground hog
that once lived under the neighbor's shed.

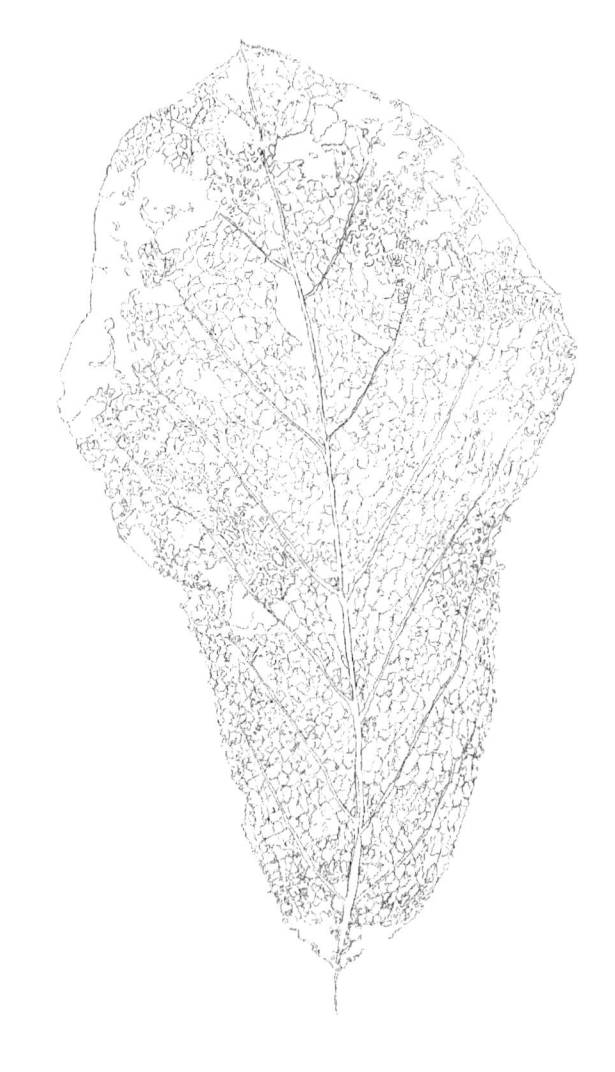

High Cirrus

Today, the curtain rose
on a high fall sky

Puffed ringlets
lining the blue cupola

Featherlike leaves
arcing gently in descent

Tomatoes blushed
by cooling nights

House sparrows
strangely silent

Foreboding in the gills
suggesting I might still be alive

Elusion

Blackberries setting
in the deepest
of reds

Meadow grass thronging
Not an inch of
bare ground

Fruit trees providing
Heavy laden
with rondure

Flowers overblooming
in orange
and blue

Earth black and rich
Crumbly
All-giving

Songbirds
Coming and going
at ease

A man clad in muslin,
Light-spun
Plain-woven

Simply wishing
He could hide in
this day

Falling Snow

I have been told
That a snowflake takes
45 minutes to fall
From its birth, 10,000 feet aloft

But today it seems to me that
The heavy wet snow is falling
Much faster than that

Serious in pace
As if no flutter will be brooked,
The flakes bring to mind the endless
Kinetic particles etched in
The celluloid of an old silent movie

Where the flow is always downward
Sucked ceaselessly through a gate

Yet behind that motion
The players in the garden are still

Never more motionless
Than when adorned with snow

Branches and twigs
Once dry and bare
Now defined
By the beauty of their garments

The ordinary pickets
And a lowly wheelbarrow
Rendered magical

While just overhead,
The geese squawking south
Are a hidden formation
Cloaked in the loamy sky
To be heard and not seen

Onset

This year's November
Has but brushed the shrubs
With frost
Guiding those companions
To colors unmatched
And lasting

Shall we not likewise
Withhold harsh touches,
Screen the wind,
Gentle our days together
Awaiting
Gray winter?

Hydrangeas

Each year I find you
Like the hydrangeas

More beautiful

More purple
Pink and
Blue

In my eyes

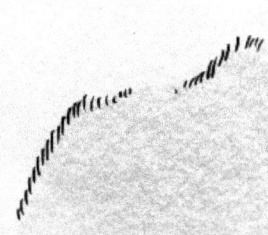

While You Sleep

Nothing through the grapevine
No whispers on the wind

The birdie didn't tell me
The clothesline wouldn't sing

Only the weeds called out,
Laughingly, mockingly
"While you sleep," they vowed

Meadow Petals

As I stepped out this morning

At half-light,
When all is going
in quiet ways

Magnolia petals
Had newly fallen
on the garden's meadow

Not so many yet
As to be a carpet
or a stream to wade through

But placed,
As if by a lover's hand,
as only the fallen can be

Mid-Epigraph

Those who make
For themselves
    A garden

        Renew
        Their devotion

Those who make
Of themselves
   A garden
      Await
      The hereafter

Hidden Flowers

I heard a rabbi say
Eve's apple was a fig

As the couple
Used fig leaves

To cover their
Pudenda

While the fig itself,
Deemed in ancient times

To be
無花果 —no flower fruit

Is in truth
內花果 —flower within fruit

For, like us,
Its flowers and processes

Are mysterious
and concealed

Gratitude

Harvesting vegetables
in my quiet garden
My thoughts turn to
your now-passed father

Whose name, Tetsuo, "Iron Man"
Testifies forever to his toughness

And I reflect on how
he was caught redhanded
90 long years ago
Stealing a cabbage
in a cold Hokkaido field

His hungry little body
Most thoroughly thrashed
by the angry farmer

Leaving him with scars
He bore for life

Today, as my hands
Cradle that same cabbage

How can I but remember
How much harder it went
for Tetsuo?
And how I wish
I could share this cabbage with him now

Culpate

Approaching the Privet
to rid it
of Strangling Honeysuckle

I cast myself forward
in the role
of Garden Defender

But the metallic "chip"
of the Mother Cardinal

like a Geiger counter
fast repeating
as I drew closer

announced that
Others
saw me otherwise:

a Nest Destroyer
Home Wrecker
Baby Killer

Marauder
and
Brigand

To Takiko

On Monday,
I wrap the blueberry bush
because you like to eat my berries

On Tuesday,
I gather turnips and shiso
to pickle them like Japan

On Wednesday,
I tie up the raspberry stems
because you dream about fruit tarts

On Thursday,
I cage the tomato vines,
to grow you the blackest krim

On Friday,
I keep the hound out back
because the peaches are for you

On Saturday,
I tug the plumpest figs
to make you sigh and smile

On Sunday,
I humbly submit to you
that I am deserving of your love

Blue

This morning
At earliest daylight
When a gardener sees
things seldom seen

I spied a catbird
Flying
With the bluest of berries
in his beak

Yet when he alighted
On a wire
I saw it was not a berry
but a shard of an eggshell

Whose cast of blue
In the moment
My eyes
failed to note

Thus, I cannot recall whether
The blue
Was catbird blue
or robin's egg blue

Whether
He was harming
the nest of another

Or experiencing
The loss
of his own

Both of which
make me his kin

MG

If I make
a Master Garden,

Am I made
a Master Gardener?

Compass Points

88° E has me pruning the winter berry
208° SW finds me nailing shingles on the shed
188° S crushing lantern flies on the snowbell's bark and
313° NW taking a leak out of sight

Naturally, also
From time to time
My fingers reach downwardly
Like roots into the clay

But as to the firmament—
The stars, moon, and occasional twinkling craft

They are like a lovely maiden, far, far away

And I simply find myself
Gazing, longing, and letting go

Taskmastering

No day in my garden passes
Without thoughts of my ancestor

With every joy
Remembrance

Diligence ruling

Sloth an affront

Most beloved—
An observant eye,
A worker's hand,
Calm,
And sturdiness

I know the birds and delight in them because of him

And remember how he once cared for me
On a particular sick day long ago

When I threw up in a bucket
Made of steel

Yet also with me
From time to time

The once acid sarcasm

Taskmastering

Minute and ungenerous
Criticism

Mocking of the fat and lame

These I rinse with the dust
Till with the clay
Pound with the fence posts

And toss in the compost

Inspiration (靈感)

Soon after
my mother passed

I was tending
the Secret Garden,

chatting with a friend
a world away

about being moved 感
by the spirit 靈,

when a crow
batted down

to join me
in the meadow.

Perilously close,
it pressed down on the air,

circling,
wheeling above my head,

giant black wings
sounding me like chimes.

"There's your poem,"
said my friend.

Bridling

I once knew a gardener whose
favorite chore was weeding
Perhaps akin to cleaning up
and keeping order

Prying each offender by the roots
For an illusion of permanence
Against entropy

Yet the Mother of All Things
is not perturbed
by what we find loathsome, and
remains indifferent to our grooming

In light of this,
the Eden of a B-movie set,
Plastic plants
Etched on celluloid
is a joke told by
a pandering, scraping
notion of God

Rather, to my mind

Eden yet bounds
an angry hornet nest
of creeping vines,
sloshing mud,
and nourishing decay

And to see God as bridled
is to paper over death

4

Four-cornered state
Four-cornered street
Four-cornered house
Four-cornered room
Four-cornered garden
Four-cornered life
Four-corneredoid

Dead Elm

When, after a strong wind storm

Dead elm twigs littered the winter garden

In contra poise to spring, when gentle winds
Merely cast the tree's progeny
To every corner of the yard

Some sticks, sent down with force,
Lodged eerily upright in the dense earth
Like totems to the tree's demise

That which could not be seen from the ground
The mushrooming process of death before the fall
Was now visible, up close, in stark relief
Minute and lovely grey and white split gills
Colonizing on the dark and crumbly bark

It was as if the elm were saying
Once again

I am here
I am here
I am not gone
I am here

Cherries

Long ago, at a wedding
Or perhaps an opening

Midge and Stanley said
We must still be in love

Because we ate
From the same plate

              This day, I harvested
                      Our cherries

      And, like the sleek gray catbird,
      Brought them home to the nest

              Feeding them to you
                      One by one

Jilted

Each year
my Autumn Joy sedum
was the belle of the ball in September
attracting more honeybees
than any other flower

Yet this year
she stood fairly untouched
perhaps a stray bee or two only
calling on her powder

Thankfully,
this was no colony collapse disorder
but rather a jilting
at the hands of the alluring shiso
grown tall and fragrant

And adorned with too many bees to count

Ode to Cai Ren Wei (蔡仁偉)

The gardener was absent
in service of
his mother's widowed husband

The peaches were unguarded
as the gardener's hound
was couchbound in the house

Yet, upon his return,
the gardener did not enter the house
nor otherwise release the hound

But instead, most unwisely,
the gardener went directly to his orchard,
a book of Chinese poetry in his hand

And there it was that the gardener
nabbed the culprit red-handed—
its bushy tail bobbing among the peach leaves

And while this loathsome motion
disgusted the gardener
and alerted him to the presence of the thief

It was not until a well-formed peach struck the ground
with a thud
and the gardener saw the ruined, half-chewed orb

That the gardener's gall rose
and, finding only poetry at hand,
vainly flung the book in anger

The gardener yet missing by a long shot
the vanishing rodent
while the book settled in fertile soil

Fore edge, book block,
cover and spine of the gardener's copy
all damaged and dirty

And because this book of poetry
could only be had in Taiwan
and was dear to the gardener

Having sounded in sympathy with
certain of the gardener's poems—
poems the dear reader finds here

The gardener sought
consolation
in knowing

That the author
of the gardener's now-soiled book,
蔡仁偉

Would surely find humor
in the gardener's
sound and fury

And how rudely flung
was the gardener's use
of his poetry

Late August Garden

A late August garden
with its undrinking leaves
and shrunken, come-too-late fruits

Signals hard thoughts
and perhaps a warning
to half-century eyes

Like a rook laid out
By a farmer in a field

Black wings placed
Just so

A piece of bright white chalk
In its mouth

The Fig King

Today I had a daydream
I had the only dell
in Pennsylvania
Mild enough to winter a ficus

And in this dell
I raised a massive
and resplendent
Fig tree

30-foot tall and 30-foot wide

Each and every year to bear
countless buckets of
purple-yellow figs

A monopoly of riches
Lovingly cartoned
People coming from miles around
Everyone bowing down to me
The one and only Fig King
Gold and silver in my pockets

Flower bud

Many a gardener
Will tell you

That a flower bud
Is still more precious than

A flower

Because a bud promises

A flower

Tumbling

My wayward father
A child of polio
Had one strong leg
The other a matchstick

And he was fond of saying
That ambulation
Was a process of falling
And righting oneself

Falling and righting oneself
In an endless ballet
Of balance and
Momentum

Yet if I were to use
A device to count
Each step I take
In the garden

The thousand times
I fall
And right myself
Each day

The device
Would not distinguish
Those special times when
I truly tumble to the ground

Untouched (song lyrics)

Has someone tied a bow
On flowers that grow
A kiss that is enclosed in a letter,

Has someone made a draught
Of a baby's soft laugh
To drink from a carafe and live better?

There's no number assigned at all
There's no policy involved
When it all becomes too much
Is there something left untouched?

When children hear the reeds
Like whispering trees
Do they feel the need to take their measure,

When raindrops hand the lake
Their glittering jade
Does she lie awake and count her treasure?

There's no number assigned at all
There's no policy involved
When it all becomes too much
Is there something left untouched?

Untouched, untouched, untouched, untouched
Untouched, untouched, untouched, untouched

Almighty

I like a plant
That bides my abuse
With leathery leaves
And iron roots

That basks in drought
And drinks in flood
Powders the ground about
With dried up blood

Male and female
Are found in its sexes
It can hold a drink in its
Solar plexus

Budding, sporing,
Dividing in time,
It's happy in loam
And happy in lime

See how it creeps
When conditions require
Or sends up runners
Climbing higher on higher

How it thrives in clay
And blooms in sand
Doesn't mind arid
Or icy lands

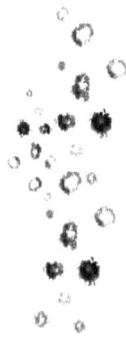

Bugs don't eat it
From what I'm told
Its flowers repel them
Like the marigold

Most frightening of all
Are its magical fruits
That are born on endless
Sturdy shoots

And its ever flowing nectar
In all seasons sweet
Its dreams are nightmares
Don't drink!

Mycology

When, after a warm spring rain
A troop of tender mushrooms popped up
By the moist corner of a raised bed

It crossed my mind
To be foolish and
Bold in my half-knowledge

And to take a nibble

But what dissuaded me
Was not just an awareness
That my ignorance could be deadly

But the dour precept that
Most mushrooms,
Like people,
Are insipid

Some are passable

Still less are delightful

And a seldom few are magic

Masculist

My peach tree's
Blossoms
And later,
Her round, full fruits,
Are subject to
My male gaze

Tender shoots
and baby greens
Bear my endearments—
Honey, sweetie, darling, to name just a few

The squirrels
Are prone to my harassment
And a hostile work environment

It's a good thing
I'm not like other men

Sunshower

Standing by the pond
Sun burning through
A gentle sheet of drops

Thunder is rumbling
Boding my father
A lover of sunshowers
Long lost

And how he stood
Just here
Somewhere else

Allies and Enemies

Are the ever-prolific beans
That kindly feed
Our family each night
Still my friends

When their probing tendrils
Grasp
A healthy tomato plant
And overrun it?

Or use
Our lovely red okra
Like a satellite
To reach closer to the sun?

Or wind about
The tender sapling peach
And begin their meddlesome ascent
To greater heights?

Keeping the peace,
I gently untwine
The spiraling coils
And scold the beans for their rapacity

"Do you think I can't grow tired of you?"

Dard

Can't lay claim to "Dad"
Can't lay claim to "Bard"

Like a garden gnome
Or pink flamingo

I will find my safe space
in stupid

And craft a portmanteau
in doltitude

Henceforth answering to
"Dard"

Menaces

When I step into the ring
That is my garden,
There is much arrayed against me—

Hungry birds, tenacious rodents, blight, and rot.

Fierce, stinging yellowjackets
Have made a home
Deep within the soft, fragrant bed of thyme.

They come and go from their tunnel
Like North Korean fighter craft
Emerging from a secret mountain lair.

And why has a past owner-ghost
Left me with those profoundly stupid,
Jagged metal rods?

Peeking up at stumble level,
They are a legacy sometimes hidden and treacherous
But always rusty and stubbornly anchored.

And did I mention flooded drought, clay, and sloth?
My addled mind doth not recall...

Uhh...

Perhaps most daunting
The gathering pain
And inflexibility of old age
And my boundless,
Ever-present capacity to hurt myself.

Yet, in light of these
I am all the more grateful
To have friends by my side—
Loyally burrowing,
Turning,
Ceaselessly shifting…

And munching on decay.

Abracadabra
Abracadabr
Abracadab
Abracada
Abracad
Abraca
Abrac
Abra
Abr
Ab
A
Ab
Abr
Abra
Abrac
Abraca
Abracad
Abracada
Abracadab
Abracadabr
Abracadabra

The hummingbirds
Play in the spray

My mother has passed
And it hurts my heart

The peaches plump
In the humid night

My father has passed
And it hurts my heart

The dragonflies
Hover above

The arc

The green beans set
Baby fruit

So fine

My parents are gone
And it hurts my heart

Cold Snap

If you plant
Your little white beans
Too early
Before a longish cold snap comes

It is best
To remain patient
'Tis likely
That nothing much will come of them

Catbirdeus Maximus

Managing my chores
in your Saville Row suit

Bitching all day—
are you a cat in heat?

Eyeing me, like I'm the bloke in
Florida's been feeding you

Flying off with my berries
Pecking down on my peaches

Doing your best
to get bad with me

Nobody ever said
you were lacking for character

Duende

Is it tidy rows of seedlings
that bring us back to the garden?

Songs of birds,
Well-honed secateurs,
Rich black soil?

Or is it
A late and sudden frost,
Finches nipping the cotyledons,
Fallen fruit, and
Promised Edens?

Cautious Wren

Yesterday, I watched a wren
At the suet feeder,
The legs and talons of his little body
Grasping the house-shaped cage.

Yet not as you might imagine—

Rather than simply
Feeding at the trough,

He clutched behind him
And faced outwardly from the house,
Like a circus strong man
Who wondrously defies
The gravity
Of his own breastweight.

Perching thus,
(As his default position),
He surveyed the environs
And seldom ventured
To turn and peck
At the nurturing block of fat,

As indeed
It exposed his back to the world
And all that
The world threatens.

Hmm…

It seemed to me that this
Most studious wren
Was intent on adhering to a principle
Reflected in my own
Advancing age:

That the survival of
Eating
Weighed less heavily
Than being eaten.

Bear Bees (熊蜂)

Like a man rich in coins
I stood by the lace cap hydrangea

And observed stout
And diligent lasses

Pollen-laden
With sticky saddlebags

Jockey and jostle each other
For nectar

Gentle, unstinging
Tireless, unstinting
Strong and unbumbling

Their Chinese name suits them—

熊蜂
(Bear Bees)

Dolly

When you grew too ungainly
For where you were raised
I took a cutting from you
And made sure you struck

Now that I've dug up
Every bit of your roots
I have replanted you
To root again

Is it you?
Or another you?
Unlike a seedling
You are not a child

Rather you are a cloned sheep
An arm or leg once planted
That grew back into
You once more

Weathered apart
Of different shape
Disjointed time
Sundered circumstance

Laddishness

As long as I have known this room,
It has been my tool garage
A beloved barracks
Where trusty battle mates
Line the walls
Ready for action
Valiantly awaiting the grasp of my hand

Yet my love for the room deepened when,
Competing buck naked within its walls
I rowed on dry ground to an old man's
American record
My stubborn ass cheeks gripping the seat
So I would not fall off
During the insane, intense
Hauling of the 100-meter sprint

And on another brilliant morning,
As I searched for an odd or end
The room became a place of spectacle
An aerial battleground
Of dogfighting cardinals
Who found themselves
Boxed in together
For a few red seconds

While just today, in a poor man's rendition
Of such pageantry
The robin came by for his daily peck
Stupidly tapping at his reflection
In the crusty side window
In a pointless effort to rid himself
Of an imaginary rival

Throughout it all
Tacked unframed to the sheetrock
An old 8 x 10 of my brother and me
Standing boldly, arms over shoulders
Bears witness to all of this laddishness

Ran (乱)

Today I took a cedar shake,
pitched it in the ground
like a sundial,

Shading a tender cutting
that had not yet grown
roots with which to drink

Just for a moment,
the cutting was the warlord Ichimonji,
while I was the pious son Saburo,

Snapping off a branch of bush clover
to shelter
my rootless, napping father

Orison

Twilight
下來
Gentle my eyes.
To all I've tended
To all I've wrought.

Dawn
起來
Let me rise.
Let me rise
Once more.

The Next Lover

Learning how to garden
is like learning how to love

Cherishing Euonymus
for her selfless disposition

while nurturing Azalea
to meet her demands

Forgiving Rose's thorns
when they prick you

and adjusting to Ivy's
domineering nature

Then,
when one day
you widow the garden

the next lover
surely will not love
as you did